FIRSTMATTERPRESS
Portland, Ore.

SOMEONE I CAN HOLD GENTLY

SOMEONE I CAN HOLD GENTLY

sky mykland

FIRSTMATTERPRESS

Portland, Ore.

Second Edition
First Printed 2022
Second Edition Published 2024

Published in the United States
by First Matter Press
Portland, Oregon

Paperback ISBN 978-1-958600-40-5

Lead Editors: Emily Moon & Ash Good
Contributing Editors: Lauren Paredes
& Caroline Wilcox Reul

First Matter Press Cohort Collaborators:
Riley Danvers, Hailey Spencer,
Sonya Wohletz & ahuva s. zaslavsky

Cover Illustration: *Bouquet*
Copyright © 2022 by Rachel Mulder
rchlmldr.com

Book design by ash good
ashgood.com

POEMS

I.

you are my mother

BIRTH TAPE [for the part of me that never wants to stop hurting]

my hands, barely high enough to reach,
grab a muffin pan fresh out of the oven
& spook backward in sudden pain.
I wail through the spiraling steam
of baked blueberries. a ghost pushes to escape
from the red skin. you are suddenly gentle,
guiding my blisters under cold water, helping me
stay there until the bumps are a cold sick yellow.
you show me how to coat the burns in medicine
& cover them in bandages. once the gauze
is taped down strong, you return to bed
& leave me with morals I learn on my own:
I need to be hurting. there is no love if I am not.

NO BREAD

I.

today we walk to the bakery
on a field trip & I hold kady's hand
like teacher told us.

kady tells me about her brother who goes to
high school & I tell her my brother goes
there too; I say mine is autistic,

& I say that means *he's in his own world*,
like you told me. you're my mom, so it's true.
I say he chews his shirt & yells & plays

super mario galaxy with me, doesn't notice
when I take his allowance & spend it
at the scholastic book fair. but then

kady says her brother
is nothing like mine. she says her brother
plays football, & I start to think,

what if I had a football brother?
I think you'd like him better if he
were your football son, right?

we walk inside the bakery & all the bread
is white because it needs to bake
before it's yummy. teacher keeps saying,

look, don't touch. the bakers slide the dough
into the oven & shovel the hot ones
onto the cooling racks. we feel the glow

of the oven's heat. kady says I'm weird
& doesn't hold my hand on the way back.
I don't know if this makes me burnt or artisan.

II.

if I mold myself after the children
who won't play with me, will they like me?
when I brush my teeth I closely examine

for crookedness. is it okay
to think I'm good if no one else does?
if I have a different answer from everyone else,

doesn't that make me fail the spelling test?
can I love myself if I'm the weird kid,
the misshapen loaf? you told me it is all so hard,

having a son with autism, & you're my mom,
so it's true. I think you love me more
because I am Normal: I have a friend.

I throttle all the wobbly parts of myself
until they are still. I search the television,
& decide a football brother would look

a lot like my brother, with a stronger chin.
a shorter haircut. a grin. someone who can explain
why the world acts the way it does:

no bread, all teeth.

[I don't ask for you to] HOLD ME

even when my sister drags a brush through the mats in my hair. it sets fire on my scalp & I complain, even though my hair is soaked with no-tears detangling spray. when you are too tired, my sister tries to act like you. she kicks a scooter to high school every day. I want to be just like her.

even when you bring home purple medicine goo and smear it between my eyes to make the scar on my nose go away. I got it jumping on the bed of our rented RV while it was driving to the forest. I'm mad when you tell me what the goo is for. I like my face like this. it looks kinda cool.

even when other moms always ask me where you are when I ride my scooter to the library & play on the playground. sometimes I say *not here*. sometimes I say *down the street at our house* & point. sometimes I argue I am old enough, you are busy enough, you love me enough, it doesn't matter.

even when you don't brush my hair or make me spaghetti or tell me it's time for bed. taking care of my brother is more important because of his autism. my brother must be angry

all the time because of his autism. he locks me in the closet
because of his autism: that's what you say when you let me out.

even when I go out on my scooter when it's getting dark to see
how many laps I can do before you call me inside.

even when I get cold & go to bed before you remember.

HUNDRED-DAY COUGH

in the autumn before I turn 10, I spend most of my time coughing so hard I can't breathe. I sit very still on the couch & try not to wake the sleeping dragon hoarding my breath.

after the doctor swabs my throat, she tells me I have whooping cough— an illness most children are vaccinated against. I ask how I got it. eventually, you say our family is sensitive to vaccines; you say brother is *vaccine damaged* & that's why he has autism, so I never got them. you'd rather I be sick than autistic. you're my mom, so you must be right.

I cry when the doctor tells me to stay home for a week, but I decide being sick isn't horrible when you read old articles from before the vaccine existed, when people used to call it the hundred-day cough; when you feed me strawberry ice cream, tea, & drops of california poppy extract.

I go back to school with my make-up homework. I leave the room whenever my throat tickles. all the other kids look at me with morbid curiosity when I cough. the school sent a pink exposure notice home in every backpack. you say we should frame ours.

my friend walks ten feet ahead of me when we'd usually walk together, so I run up & ask why. she says, *you don't have vaccines, & my mom said my baby brother could die if he gets sick.* she runs away. I bite the inside corner of my lip until I can taste iron from the indentation. when we drive home, I stay quiet instead of letting the blood spit from my tongue. I don't know what you'd say if I blamed you. I don't want to find out.

SIMILARITIES [between you & the moon]

your affection
wanes & waxes. I look at
the moon sometimes & realize I
haven't seen her illuminated in
a while. I can't change how both
of you leave me alone to become
new in the sun. I think about
where the moon will go when
the earth bursts into flame. I
think about you & the
moon, & how

you flew to a
hospital in another country
& returned, weak, with a metal
band I cannot see. call it space
station, call it appetite constrictor.
it's made by man & it's everything
you wanted. I look at myself in the
mirror & try to remember how
much I love things that are
soft & kind.

we go to lunch
& you flip your torso
upside-down to get the food in
your digestive system unstuck:
a new chance to give yourself
sustenance. haven't you seen
the moon wane before? did
you know she'll always do it
again? in the parking lot
you tell me:

you never
wanted to be a mother to
a child so sad, so ungrateful.
it's impossible to learn (& learn
& learn) myself so unloved & still
want to struggle through another
orbit. I wish you both could be
closer, even though we've shared
every universe. when I
was very young,

I promised
myself, if you died, I
would have to die too.
I couldn't imagine continuing
this endless celestial pirouette
without you as a point in the
distance to fix my gaze on.
your orbit continues, but your
gravity is weaker now: pulls
tides & nothing more.

I've learned
never to trust
that you've grown
for good. I have to
focus on the
stars.

II.

you are my first love

OPEN MOUTHS

home is a draining hourglass, so I leave for the midnight movie.
you are in the winding ticket line again & you introduce
yourself as all I've wanted. I laugh & apologize to
the future. you intersect my timeline like a
hurricane. the night sky swallows me.
stars blink out all at once. to start
loving you, I bury a pistol in
the ground & wait for
it to bear fruit.
you bite
my
neck
instead of
waiting with
me, say you're
not in the mood to go
soft tonight, & I cry into
your shoulder all the same; drain
myself of any strength left. when you
spin the world, I break. after all the glass is
swept into the trash, we pluck the bullets from the
tree I grew & throw them into one another's open mouths.
the shells bounce against my lips, but you swallow every last one.

THE NIGHT I FALL IN LOVE

your skin tastes like an empty room in a new house.
all I want is to move in. I hear rain at the window,

so I say, it's raining outside. you move the curtain aside
& point to the noise machine. you sleep to this false flood

every night. the field in my body feels green,
growing, lush, after an eternity of yellow

brittle straw, burrs poking the soles of my feet.
you grip a tendon in my neck between your front teeth

to hear me stifle a yelp. you laugh & roll us
across the thermal blanket so the entire weight

of your bird bones presses into me. limbs sink into bedding,
malleable as my inexperienced lips on yours.

suddenly, you pull away. interrogate. *why don't you cry?*
you were sad about getting stood up.

that's why you came here. why aren't you crying?

my face is fogged over, & you are determined
to see through its cloud. I stutter through

the unfamiliar spit in my mouth, confused,
& your bite stops me. it feels like half my neck

is in your mouth. you carve & suck, painfully,
until a pricking wet feeling in my eyelids greets

like an old friend. you smile against my skin;
controlling the weather; electrified. I lose my grip on time.

one second, I feel your jaw tense harder,
& the next, my chest convulses with a salty hurricane

of catharsis. your wiry arms haul me closer,
pulling your mouth off my skin. I'm scared of how much

I want this unforecasted cradling. you murmur,
I'm here, I've got you, you're safe, it's okay.

yes, I think the drought is over. now I can feel the storm.

BREAKFAST

on one of our best days,
we both skip class,
      bacon sizzles on the stovetop.
      sun glares through the windows.

you are the one who teaches me how to cook.
      I love you for how you know to pour the meat grease in a jar.
if you love me, it's for reasons I don't quite understand.

we are friends in the way of:
cooking together, you always know more than me,
      & commend yourself.

sitting on the kitchen island,
      you list off all the people
            you could hook up with if you wanted to,
                  including me offhandedly,
I say nothing,
& in this way we are both so fragile & ignore the places
      we are breaking.

we are friends in the way the eggshells are unbroken
        & this is why I view it like there are a finite number
                        of mornings,
                        of good days.
bacon doesn't sizzle when it burns.
we run out of fruit to cut.

we are friends in the way oil pops off the pan,
        then cyclically lands on the hot metal once again,
but eating breakfast with you sustains me— small kindnesses
over the now midday light.

maybe I should care that when there aren't small kindnesses,
there are slammed doors

& maybe what you really teach me
is every way I can digest myself from the inside out.

maybe we're always burning

what matters is that I am learning the way eggs cook:
when they can't bear the heat anymore, they solidify.

YOU TELL ME [you think I'm autistic]

while I'm turn signaling out of an exit-only lane on highway 1.
when I don't listen, your words roll down the windows
& become cold, biting air so I have to listen when you say
I just thought maybe you could be— because your siblings
are autistic, right? & your dad? & you don't know
when I'm joking. you can't tell when I want you to leave.
last week, my mom said my sister might be, but that I definitely
am not. I have to trust my grip, or I will crash.
you have to understand why I can't listen.
my mom said I make friends & talk to strangers,
so I must be Normal. she called me Normal,
so I have to believe I can be or I'll crash.
you have to understand, in order to keep driving,
I have to believe I am Normal, synonym for lovable,
synonym for good, synonym for you wanting me here.
my navigation is off. hasn't shown me the end of this road,
so it doesn't exist yet. weak with the speed, I ask,
why didn't you just tell me to leave?

ONCE I TRUST

you become my home. without you I'd be unmoored,
so I hold on, grinding down on the traction of my bootsoles.

when you decide you've learned everything about me,
the last lockpins slide & I pop open. for you, the fun is over.

I don't remember being anywhere but in your gripping hands.
you say you're bored, so you can justify hitting me

once as a joke, then twice more to laugh.
you say I hit you back, so you can hit me again, harder.

you say my having emotions about this is weak.
some days, you are the last water slipping through my fingers.

I go through life parched, not in the aftermath of war, but in the
withdrawal, red eyes & shaking isolation. I would

do anything to go back to when it was good— that night
together, goosebumps on my ribcage, sorrow in my gut,

you holding me tighter than anyone but my mother had.
maybe that was closer than we should have ever been.

I keep believing you will come back, nicer than you ever are.
I hear your laughter in a crowd & turn around.

when I hear doors open, I always check if it's you.
you hold my heart in your hands & twist,

then say it's my fault for handing it over in the first place.
I practice not loving you every day.

HURTING & HELPING

a long time ago
my neighbor & I went out to play in
her yard.
her german shepherd
was tearing into her leashed
poodle's neck.
all blood & hot panic,
trying to escape from the fence.
I was told
the big one—
escaping from captivity,
just wanted to free
the small one
from the fence

I mean,
fighting is normal.
desperately wanting to escape

is something we can
understand.

that doesn't mean
this
tangy blood
was wrong,
can you understand
why?

it feels like I met you

for some reason

maybe you were
supposed to help me,

there are reasons you could be:
you love me, but don't separate

me from my imperfections.
I still miss you, hopping down
to sit & watch dogs
& people walk by;
their wisdom, unknown to me.
maybe this
powerlessness is what I am

forgetting on purpose
naively

believing
what you tell me is true.
love, this innocence, this
shower of affection
scares me for some reason
I don't know

HOW TO BLOW OUT A CANDLE [or, how to leave you & then return in seven steps]

1. blow it out.

2. watch the smoke.

3. when the smoke continues to wind up, blow on it more. my air seems to be feeding you— it, the candle— fueling it with my breath. stop blowing, then resume, but this time just to see the red wick glow; just to wonder how a thing that smells so good, looks so pretty, treats me so well, can also burn down my house.

4. don't stop watching, the unattended spark could catch— think about how horrible it is that something so bright becomes dark so quickly, & how it was my fault. I think about how if not blown out, the candle would have consumed all its wax, or about how unattended fire is hazardous, but no, really, I miss the fire. the days when I was simply in love with the glow, how you flickered back then. I miss the nights that were cold, when I usually was warmed by the flame. you felt like the home I'd searched for, the tongues of your flame flicked against my neck, burned me alive.

5. watch the spark fade into black & panic. reach for survival
   & find only frigid air.

6. fumble with matches & relight the candle.

7. skip fingers through the flame & burn them by getting
   too close over & over & over. consider how they are tender.
   repeat.

RABBIT HOLES ARE NOT HOMES

we tip back peach vodka mixed with gatorade.

alice in wonderland flickers on the television,
      & bridger teaches me to hold my breath when I take shots
      to make them easier to swallow.

we talk about the rabbit hole
      & you,
            who has one for a mouth.

bridger was there when we split the court apart with our yelling,
      couldn't decide who to follow afterwards.
tells me
      you wondered out loud if you spat me out too harsh;
      if trial should have come before sentence.

      you talked to bridger about painting fifteen roses.
I say it's always been foolish to poison the flowers;
you probably shouldn't waste the paint.

we are not natural,
      & neither are our roses.

alice drinks from a vial, shrinks into a tiny, tiny girl.
I feel so small,
hold my breath, &

swallow.

GEOMETRIC PROOF [for why I lie awake thinking of you]

Statement	Reason
1. I am born.	**Given.**
2. I experience childhood neglect: learn to unlock the door, cook my own food & tuck myself in.	**Given.**
3. I grow up. My dad tells me he can still see ways I haven't changed since childhood.	**Reflexive Property:** Me = Me; neglected child is congruent to an adult who always seems to write it off as "not that bad, I survived, after all."
4. I met you. I fell in love with you, inequality a constant, stronger in theory. The problems you present feel like a review.	**Transitive Property:** If I, as a child, was neglected, & I am congruent to myself, then I as an adult must also be forgotten, ignored, misplaced & abused. A = B & B = C, so A, must also, = C.

5. I keep you in my life, despite how you hurt me. At sixteen, I tell my mother & she does nothing.	**Symmetric Property:** If this is the same timeline, & things were already like this, then they must continue. If 1 = 1 in 2006, 1 = 1 now too. Past = Present, so Present is also = to Past.
6. I go to therapy & start loving myself more than hating what I still can't understand.	People were never math problems to begin with.
7. I stop seeing relationships like equations. Love doesn't add or subtract based on how I think I was weird last night; it builds over time & craves companionship like sustenance.	There doesn't always have to be a reason, but

8. I can't stop seeing you in certain places. You know them too: my self-hatred, the part of me that doubts, those nights when I just can't shake thinking about how you have done good things & bad things, but despite how a positive infinity added to a negative infinity is zero, to me you are nowhere near neutral.	You are not the sum of your actions, you are all of them together because people are not just a collection of numbers to be added, but that means I have no idea where to place you, with no reasoning, theorems, or properties to help me. I hate you, but I love you. You don't have to prove your toxicity to me, & I still have all the hurt. However, continuing to struggle at understanding the same question is frustrating, & I got lost.
9. As a problem, you broke me: my scratched-out midnight calculations stretch over every memory.	To solve you, I have to accept I will never find the answer.

III.

you are my best friend

THE NIGHT I MEET YOU

you convince everyone at the party
to put on the worst movie I've ever seen,
but argue against a drinking game, say if we took shots
every time the director made an actress enter the scene,
nipples clearly visible through her shirt,
we'd all get alcohol poisoning.
I slip away to the kitchen to make mac & cheese
from my mom's cupboard. as the water boils, you walk in,
(say *it's almost over, & I've already seen it like fifty times)*
grab the spoon with long fingers & stir.
your grin makes a dimple cave near your jaw.
my face feels warm. I ask if I look sunburnt,
& you consider me, one eyebrow raised.

FIRSTS

five minutes after you tell me you've never bleached your hair
but want to, I turn the key to drive us to the beauty store.
over a tiled floor, I brush your wavy hair with careful fingers.
this interweaving is a tender revelation.
bleach mixture stirred, I balance one knee
on your thigh, messily section your hair
with a tie peeled from your wrist. I would spend another lifetime
pulling my fingers through lush golden brown,
so soft it feels pretend. when brush bristles scrape
the bottom of the tupperware, only half your curls
are saturated with the purple foam.
you are not the girl I was in love with last year.
we agree we'll laugh tomorrow.

twenty-five minutes later, lukewarm water
baptizes brassy mismatched locks, your head flipped
upside-down, eyes wrinkled shut. when you open
the bathroom door, you've styled a benediction
out of a botched blessing. my gaze is hungry prayer.
your smile, the rusty inside of a secret.

the numbers on the clock grow larger than their past
until they are small again. my garage-turned-bedroom is

dark except for where we lay, knees bumping, hand in hand,
canopied by purple string lights. harmonies on the speaker
name heartbreak a hurricane.

when you ask if I would kiss any of my friends,
I don't answer at first, giggling, then carefully fit my hand
around your hip. I look back up to learn
exactly how long your eyelashes are.

I don't know you're a girl yet. still think I am, somehow.
I press fingers into the pulse point on your neck,
& you suck in the air from my lungs;
I learn your heartbeat's rhythm, how it gets faster
when you kiss me. I move to hold the drum in my teeth.
your lips become bloodless, icy with wanting.
after, still naked, we gently map skin;
agree in soft voices we would switch bodies if we could.

when we let outside air back into the windowless room,
the drowsy sunrise blinds us.
surprised, sleepless laughter swallows us back into my bed—
we can't expose how we spent this night.
not to this dawn. not yet.

ALL HORNS ALL HALO

I get out of the shower &
laugh, then can't stop.
you'll understand eventually.
you lied about fucking me to
your boyfriend. he
texted me, & I should be mad.
instead,
still dripping from the shower,
I'm staring at myself in the mirror,
mechanical chuckle,
untamed eyes scouring
these bright reflections,
slippery with gloss.
I wrap my body
a torn puzzle piece
sometimes, or a bathtub,
filled with
shattered glass.
you make me heal, as well as hurt,
heartstrings pulling
the day after I find out
you apologize.
I look at you, but
everything is changing.

tell me
& I'll listen,
I'll believe you
show me again how
to know I'm foolish

sometimes, I love you so much I
spend time thinking you are holy;
you look at me too gentle, but

my head is filled with sand.
I realize
all

my thoughts about you:
they are glitter fake,
I want it to feel real when
around you, I think you are
completing me

a full sip of
understanding:
a requiem of
fingernails across my scalp.
I drive you to school.
sometimes—
no, mostly, I watch the road
sometimes the leaves,
sometimes you.
everything is okay now,
but I can't promise
tomorrow, or forever.
it's important
to love you, today.

WHEN YOU SAY [I think you're my best friend]

[my first thought is]

[I say]

oh fuck oh shit no I can't do this again feels like grief feels like a bog in my stomach feels like everything I wanted feels like I found a harbor that I'll never want to sail from feels like maybe I shouldn't dock at all feels like feels like feels like *please I love you so much* it feels like my love for you has always been washing over us like the tide wrapping me tightly with the memory of how you holding me feels like the safest waters feels like the sweetest wind feels like the only place I can predict the tides of— I'm so happy you always see past this worn hull see how strong I am to hold up the decks of my pupils to meet yours— your smile is my lighthouse & I cannot ignore the cold or my

...

...

...

...

oh shit,

really?

well, yeah. hunger any longer & if I had lied & said *no* you would have seen the truth in my finicky fingers stumbling to tie the sails in how my soft spots for you bridge the ocean feels like feels like feels like they always will.

. . .

I think you're mine too.

YOU ASK ME [if I might be autistic]

& I ask,
like, in a bad way?
then apologize.

your soft words
build around
what you've hypothesized for a long time.

I stumble on the last step of my brain's dark staircase,
tumbling forward into free online assessments,
you holding my other hand.

it may be my body, but I did not build it:
there are winding side hallways
I can only navigate when it's freezing
or the water-logged floorboards will collapse.
the lightbulbs inside locked closets
burned out a long time ago.
I open one, then shut my brother's
scream back inside.
when I yelled & called him names
he showed me how

to love someone like paint,
soaking into the walls of this life.

you call my name,
bring me back into my bedroom body,
where the laptop is open
& the scores are highlighted in yellow.

I don't dare ask how you can love me,
knowing all the repairs to be done.
you answer anyway,
promising I'm no flawed construction.
I am somewhere to call home.

IT'S NOT THAT I DON'T BELIEVE
[people love me]

I think my heart sometimes just has a leak. I haven't been taught how to patch it myself. I try to hide the sharp edges of life: top shelf of my closet, under my pillow, on my phone in an application I never open. when I left my first love, I had to remember how to use each of my organs without her. an old photo *[a group, all dressed up in front of the theater, her arm awkwardly wired around me]* surprises me with its serration. you must understand, then, why I'm stifling apologies before they leave my mouth; you must, because you let one of your own spill— *I'm sorry I don't know what to say*— while you hold me, fit your fingers under my hair. I am learning how to say *I love you* & also mean *I trust you to love me*. I try to calm my pulse when I do.

RIPTIDE

when you dreamt of them, they caught you like riptide;
pulled you from safety in their inescapable vortex.

they rolled you through the waves
while the ocean spat sand & whispered

you might never be loved again.
you hesitated before refusing.

riptides either leave you to dry in the hot sand
or replace all the air in your lungs,

so when you found yourself
separated from saltwater

opening your crusted eyes
delirious on an unfrequented shore

you always knew this had to end,
coughing your aching lungs onto the beach.

eat or be swallowed,
but you were both swept out of your depth.

RIPTIDE, RETOLD

when you dreamt of them, I have to confess, I was dreaming of you.
some distorted version of your mouth told me you'd love me
if I tucked the tags into my shirts,
&, shameful, I'd reach to my neck each morning.

your eyes start to have a faraway glint.
smiles blush your face.

unknowingly in tandem, riptide stays up all night.
they knock on my door as the wind whips
rain & debris across our windows.
sitting on the hard floor of my bedroom,
they accidentally admit their heart is with yours.

a moon cycle passes, & I say nothing.
late at night, during chess, you tell them:

my rook takes yours. did you know I'm already underwater?

nothing is new anymore when we all eat at the same table.
I hear the two of you fucking & turn up the playlist the two
of us made.

while you're in their arms, your distance from the shore grows.
I watch, hiding my mouth in a coffee cup. when a sunrise
crests your face at breakfast, I know the waters are clear.
I don't know how to say I'm worried when I've never seen you happier,
but you lose yourself to the tide every stormy night.
each time your heart breaks, it washes up on the beach.

riptide tells me you lied to them, & they're just sand now.
dried & still teeming with life.

nothing is new in this house.
both of you commiserate to me about the other.
I try to count the number of times
I've fallen for you; try to tell you,
always overdue & under my breath.

you yearn for their touch.
you will always be farther than I want you to be,
but at least you are on the shore again.
at least you are safe again.
at least loving you is more than I ever thought I'd deserve.
the glint in your eyes is faraway.
nothing is new.

IN THE PITH [of bitter longing]

I can't tell you how much I love you.

~~your hands dance when you talk, & you walk with fire. your steps rise like steam, & nothing can stop your determined momentum, & this is~~

~~this is~~

~~when you look at me I wonder~~

~~my mouth stays still~~

~~the sun warms your turned up face as I suck the juice from a slice of orange.~~

I can't tell you how much

~~some days I want to tell you. others, I want to mail every pen in the house to my future self, five years from now. roll up these pages & burn them, curling remnants floating away.~~

~~I have to remember this before I look too long.~~

~~do you think the time will ever be right for us?~~

~~do you think~~

~~do you know if~~

~~do you feel what I have felt?~~

~~do you see me, or only think you do?~~

~~spend a year in the pith of the orange, never tasting the juice,~~
~~& call it good. call it the only thing we have ever known. call it~~
~~the bitterest I've bitten, & I will disagree, but I do know that~~

I can't tell you

~~or everything will rot.~~

[poem in which I, earth, get too close to]
YOU, THE SUN

you tell me I need to stop living for the licks
I get of your warmth.
I need to accept this as gospel;
nothing less.

when the forests catch fire
I burn them into my tongue.

I am a simple rock floating in your orbit,
struggling to sustain life.

you ask me for space,
so I put millions of miles between us:
move continents, cause earthquakes, push tsunamis.

when the atmosphere chills between us,
the climate changes in our living room.
I put on an ozone layer to stop the shivers,
try to remember what you would say to my world falling apart,

but sea lines rise from my tears.
organisms fall like sand through my fingers.

everything is cold.
I feel arctic when I check if your face is pointed to me, and it is not.

I float in this galaxy, alone but for you & the moon.
anything I had before this was reborn in a bang.
I try not to blame myself for orbiting the nearest warm thing.

I know, to survive, I need to keep moving;
practice holding my gravitational pull within my sphere,
compromise my boundaries for no gods in these stars,
but my dependency has been astronomically prologued.

this vastness of how much I care is terrifying,
even to me,

but you remind me varying distances are okay.
there are no other planets like me in this galaxy;
no other stars like you in my life.

you love everything I am, even when we are at apoapsis.

& even if I turn too bleak to support my ecosystems,
or am hit by another comet of extinction,

I'll cherish your warmth,
& keep loving you back.

I SHOULD SAY YES [but don't]

1.
you ask, *have you ever had a jenny?* as the lead of the studio
killers sings about loving her best friend.
I don't tell you.

2.
in autumn, we measure our chests to get our bra sizes. I ask if
it's okay to touch your ribs. you reply, *I've literally been inside*
you, & we laugh. some days I am nothing but the blush that
crawls up my cheeks.
I don't think I'll ever tell you.

3.
this moth in my gut will die if it sees light.

4.
one morning, snow covers our house, takes out our electricity.
we light the stove with a match to make blueberry pancakes, but
I flip them too soon, make a gooey folded mess, so you laugh &
take the spatula. it's okay— I am still holding the moth inside. we
cover two pages of my notebook in hangman. I go to check if the
water from the sink downstairs is still dirty & brown. when you
hear me coming, you flip pages back to center, but I don't see.

darkness finds cider bottles in our fingers, glass reflecting candlelight; our eyelids begin drooping as we reminisce about girlfriends, high school parties, old memories. then, your smile stills. fades. eyes suddenly wide open, you stare at the bracelets on your wrist twisting around your index finger instead of my face.

you glance at my notebook, still folded open on the table, & confess.

. . . so sorry, I know it was a huge invasion of privacy. . . I didn't mean to find it, but. . . the details you wrote. . . thought we were past this. . . need to know if the love poem was about me. . .

the moth flutters, fights for freedom. my brain rushes with blood, trying to figure out which thought, which line, which pen mark led us here.

you ask if I have feelings for you like you'd ask if the house was on fire.

how could I ever tell you we're standing in the ashes?

I BELIEVE [people love me]

so, on my first good day in four months, I open my dresser
drawer. I wear my good day on my body, my earlobes, trace it
onto my eyelids. I put on headphones & set my shoulders back;
bandage anything leaking blood & text you a warcry.
under the red floodlights, your fingers pluck up & down the
instrument's spine. you wave at me when the last notes fade.
I smile wide, all eye crinkle & no blush. I'm the loudest applause,
your biggest fan, all alone in the back of the bar until I walk
forward & talk to every person who lends me their glance.
there is a song you & I sing in harmonies on long drives. for four
months, we've skipped it. tonight in my car it plays loud—
"let us be sevente-e-een / if we've still got the ri-i-ight," our
anthem echoing of the way we met, reckless, secrets hidden
under fingernails, mouths pressed without thought.
we are the echo of soft hair & thousands of conversations.
I don't know how to explain, but my heart feels even more full
harmonizing with you now, grinning & singing loud, than any
time blood has rushed through my veins at your touch.

IV.

you are me

FUNGUS [a mobius poem]

you don't exactly know how   →   the fungus found you growing
the fungus found you growing   when you were too young
when you were too young   to remember everything
to remember everything   you wrote in a log
you wrote in a log   every time you cried
every time you cried   a tally mark
a tally mark   when you scraped your knee
when you scraped your knee   you kept track
you kept track   when your dad yelled
when your dad yelled   you slammed your door
you slammed your door   & recorded
& recorded   the spreading fungus
the spreading fungus   searches for dead things in you
searches for dead things in you   to devour all of
to devour all of   a child
a child   still growing
still growing   the fungus
the fungus   wants to live
wants to live   in harmony
in harmony   & harmed
& harmed   you grew
you grew   in spite of

in spite of   what tried to consume you

what tried to consume you   except the fungus?

accept the fungus   when it tries to live

when it tries to live   just like you

just like you   it eats

it eats   the part of you

the part of you   still a child

still a child   you take pills

you take pills   in your dark bedroom

in your dark bedroom   when your face crumples

when your face crumples   your mom leaves to be alone

your mom leaves to be alone   don't keep a log

don't keep a log   now

now   you're crying too much

you're crying too much   stop asking her

stop asking her   if you're loved

if you're loved   ↺   you don't exactly know how

SAD  LIBS

Today you woke up & felt _____, so you _____

EMOTION   VERB

_____. Yesterday was too

UNHEALTHY COPING MECHANISM

_____, & tomorrow is soaked into the

ADJECTIVE

mirror when you look at _____, applying

NOUN

_____, continuing to feel _____.

BRAND OF MAKEUP   EMOTION THAT WORRIES

YOUR LOVED ONES

_____ sends you to voicemail, but this is

NAME OF FRIEND

okay because of _____. There is a reminiscence

REASON

about _____ someone, & it still _____

VERB ENDING IN —ING   VERB ENDING IN —S

you up during _____. Your therapist tells you

TIME OF DAY

_____, & you think you're

IDIOM

supposed to feel _____, but you don't. This weighs
EMOTION

on you with the weight of a _____. Sometimes you
NOUN

_____ as you drive your_____
EMOTIVE VERB   VEHICLE

& at these times you often wonder who's in more danger: you,

or the people around you. For hours, you stare at _____
COLOR

pages, tracing _____ like _____, like
PLURAL SHAPE   PART OF A FIRE

_____ is _____ down your
BRAND OF MAKEUP   VERB ENDING IN —ING

face & _____ can't do anything to help.
NAME OF PERSON
IN ROOM

Some days, you are like _____ , always
HISTORICAL FIGURE

burning, living, writing, _____, & other
VERB ENDING IN —ING

days you think you are like _____
RELIGIOUS FIGURE

best known for how _____ died. You wonder what you'll be
PRONOUN

known for: _____ or _____.
VERB ENDING IN —ING   VERB ENDING IN —ING

Will you be remembered for your _____ or
MENTAL ILLNESS

your _____? Will something inside of
ART FORM

you always feel blank?

STRONGLY WORDED LETTER
[to my past self]

you moisturize with old pictures & text messages.
replay videos again & again & again.
you stuff every good memory into black donation bags,
& they sit in the trunk of your mind for months.
when you remember, you reluctantly open the hatch
& find it all mildewed, tunneled through
by little brown moths.

at a party, someone says a name you never hear anymore
but always think about, & you bum a cigarette just to
smell like smoke. frown just to be asked if you're okay.
leave just to know you'll be worried about. at home,
you dream of when things were still good
& try to recreate it every night. in the morning,
you savor the stab of remembering where you are.

what hurts you most is when the scalding email
to everyone at work is clearly about you,
& you're out of food to cook but also too broke to get take-out,
even when you lay on the decrepit trampoline
in the backyard & tearfully look at the stars,
no one notices until you say something.

doctors pathologize you, sitting stiffly on leather couches.
a friend confesses in detail why they love you,
& you offer the memory to the moths.

sure, I hear you. at the age you were supposed to be coddled,
you learned to use the stovetop alone. sure,
you still have the scar between your eyes,
& the one on your right eyebrow, & another next to your
hairline.

you sink into your self-pity, but never seem to drown.
it doesn't matter if I decide whether I want you to live or die.
you always wash ashore,
coughing up a new plan to survive.

HELP

when you & your loved ones promise
each of you will talk about it if a pill bottle
starts to look like an open door,
sign names with a pen running out of ink,
you don't realize everyone else means it fully.
you answer any calls late into the night,
but you fall to your knees before asking
for a reprieve.

you turn the pages of the same book:
identical breakdowns.
you try to find a place
where honesty can coexist with comfort.
you know trust is their greatest mediator,
but the two of you only ever talk for a moment
before trust checks her watch.

when you can't see light above
& the car key in your hand becomes darker than the sky,
you ask the girl you trust more than blood to help.
she saves your life again, gently;
lays it back on your shoulders like holy shawl;

continues as your deliberately unsung salvation.
you leave to save her in turn.

last time, you swore you'd feel better,
so you would never return
to the flashing red lights & sirens.

on the road to your crumbled promise,
you tongue around your mouth for sores.
play every song you know you'll miss.
she says she loves you at the end of every sentence.
you are realizing you have to sing your own benediction;
you say a prayer when you wake, tongue holding up the sky.

AVIARY

you call to
explain they are letting the
birds from the cage. something
about nature healing. the man sitting
in front of you who thinks he is God wraps
three white linen blankets around himself in
manic devotion. pray for nameless salvation for
the first time you can remember. if you get too close
to a bird, it will either peck out your eyes or name
you its mother. at least, that's what God told you. you
drew the 3 of spades from his deck at 3:45 am & He
told you it meant you should plant a garden. you only
have seeds. every bird you eat, straight from the vine,
increases your drive. you will start composting. you
will walk every day. this will be your grace. for every
God who has touched you, every doctor, every cure,
your wingspan is clipped until it grows again. then,
resume search for your flock, for any savior moist with
your spit, for any animal lined up for slaughter. you
often consider that if you were a bull, you would be
hamburger age; the age of being alive, fully grown, but
not too chewy; aged, like the voicemail you reach; like
the message, you leave; the birds, they are coming.

[an incomplete guide to accepting you are]
AUTISTIC

in summer, tell your psychiatrist
about how the world is too bright
& warm & loud. she will casually
invert your memories. refer you to a phone number.
after you hang up that video call, remain still,
curl into yourself, stare at the wall for minutes.
you won't know why.

you don't have to tell everyone right away.
you don't have to tell anyone, actually.

meanwhile, every time you break
one of your strategies to be loved—
[don't talk too much don't ask weird questions
don't stare don't leave awkward silences
don't breathe too loudly from your mouth]—
the moment plays under your eyelids,
rubbing fists, seeing stars.
imagine if your apologies
weren't on a hair trigger.

leave the party when the music
blasts into an ear & tries
to escape through your skull.

your mom will call. don't answer.
when you begin thinking through the words to tell her,
your mouth drops into your gut.

walk down the stairs & shake the tension
from your wrists in time with the steps.
realize you've walked down the stairs
like this, while alone, since you were very small.
you've always held your hands still when someone is close.

decide it's okay to eat oatmeal five times in two days,
& when you worry that's weird,
remind yourself that Normal
is scratchy intolerable fabric
to pull on & never fits, anyway.

SOFTLY WORDED LETTER [to my past self]

I'm so proud of you.
every day, I tell you in the morning,
as I pry the blanket off our head one fold
at a time, as gently as I can.

for years, you've pictured yourself
locked in a death match with your sadness.
someday, you might realize you owe it an apology:
depression has always wanted you
more than you wanted yourself.
it simply wants to keep you safe, wrapped in softness,
always away from the scalding of the past.

you're learning how to love yourself
without a declaration from someone else:
rolling the windows down, turning up the volume,
feeling the freeway rushing through your hair.
you sing along, not to hear your voice,
but to feel the music in your teeth.
you're celebrating your own wins, alone, exuberant.

you treat love like a scavenger hunt falling to chaos,
a competition with rules always changing.

my youngest self, the part of me still primal
& hurting, I want to tell you
about how you survived.

you don't know any better, so I teach.

you deserved better, & I will tell you this every day.

ACKNOWLEDGMENTS

As someone who was a fiercely independent child & now an adult still learning how to accept support, I briefly considered thanking no one. My default mentality is still often to draw in rather than reach out. That said, the following people were simply too good to me & too important for this book's development to not thank.

A hearty thank you to:

Ash Good, Emily Moon, Lauren Paredes, Sonya Wohletz, Caroline Wilcox Reul, Hailey Spencer, & all of First Matter Press for their gentle & meticulous handling of these poems.

Rachel Mulder. You & your work are such a joy to experience, & I'm so glad your art is on my debut's cover.

My best friend for the ridiculous levels of support & understanding she's gifted me. I'm not naming her in the interest of her privacy, but she knows who she is, profoundly & in more ways than one.

The members of Mouth House. I wrote pretty much this entire book while living in our little community; the effects of the collective neurodivergent queer artist vibes on my thoughts & words are as permanent as our matching tattoos of teeth.

Everyone who has held my words weekly in the poetry communities of Santa Cruz, California & Portland, Oregon.

My long-standing therapist.

Google Drive. Couldn't have done it without you, babe.

The poems "open mouths" & "rabbit holes are not homes" were previously published by *Selcouth Station* in March 2022.

An earlier version of the poem "similarities [between you & the moon]" was published by *Fifth Wheel Press* as "similarities [between the moon & my mother]" in July 2022.

CONTENT WARNINGS BY POEM

Page 3, "birth tape"
burn injury; mention of childhood neglect

Page 4, "no bread"
ableism toward autistic people; allusion to internalized
ableism about autism

Page 7, "hold me"
childhood neglect; ableism toward autistic people; mention
of head injury

Page 9, "hundred-day cough"
description of pertussis (whooping cough); anti-vaccine
rhetoric; ableism toward autistic people

Page 11, "similarities"
mention of gastric band weight-loss surgery; suicidal
ideation & description of negative parental response to
suicidal ideation

Page 17, "open mouths"
allusion to speaker's neck being bitten in an intimate way

Page 18, "the night I fall in love"
description of consensual kissing and speaker's neck being bitten in an intimate way

Page 20, "breakfast"
mention of emotional abuse

Page 22, "you tell me"
negative reaction to autistic traits; internalized ableism about autism

Page 23, "once I trust"
non-graphic mention of physical abuse

Page 25, "hurting & helping"
description of an animal being injured by another animal

Page 29, "rabbit holes are not homes"
mention of alcohol

Page 31, "geometric proof"
brief mentions of childhood neglect & physical abuse

Page 37, "the night I meet you"
mentions of alcohol, underage drinking & misogyny

Page 38, "firsts"
non-explicit description of sexual activity

Page 40, "all horns // all halo"
brief mention of previous sexual activity

Page 47, "riptide"
description of drowning as part of a metaphor

Page 48, "riptide, retold"
brief mention of sexual activity

Page 52, "you, the sun"
description of codependency

Page 55, "I should say yes"
brief mention of previous sexual activity & alcohol

Page 61, "fungus"
psychiatric medication; mention of childhood emotional abuse & neglect

Page 63, "sadlibs"
allusion to suicidal ideation

Page 66, "strongly worded letter"
mentions of cigarette smoking & childhood neglect

Page 68, "help"
suicidal ideation; allusion to ambulances & medical care

Page 70, "aviary"
allusion to being in a psychiatric hospital

Page 71, "autistic"
internalized ableism about being autistic

SKY MYKLAND is a neurodivergent, nonbinary lesbian poet and self-proclaimed special occasion, currently based in Portland, OR. When they're not writing poetry, you can find them Googling "androgynous outfits," walking dogs, applying for public assistance, and thinking about poetry. Follow them at @xylophonepoetry on Instagram and Twitter, or find more of their work at xylophonepoetry.com.

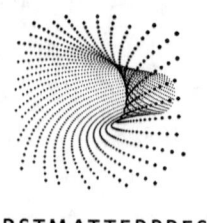

FIRSTMATTERPRESS
Portland, Ore.

First Matter Press is a collective press in Portland, Oregon, founded in 2018 to dissolve publication barriers for first-time publishing poets and genre-expanding writers. Our annual releases center community and craft by inviting authors into a creative cohort where they crystallize manuscripts in dialogue with editors and fellow writers and collaborate with featured artists on original cover art.

We are a 501(c)(3) non-profit organization and our authors maintain 100% copyrights and sales royalties of published work. Find our titles at IndieBound.org, Powells.com, BN.com and other major bookseller websites.

2022
FEATURED COVER ARTIST RACHEL MULDER

FIRSTMATTERPRESS.ORG

2021
FEATURED COVER ARTIST ALEKSANDRA APOCALISSE

CONSIDER THE BODY, WINGED
jessica e. pierce

ROUTES BETWEEN RAINDROPS
dan wiencek

THE GROWTH LINES
gabby hancher

2020
FEATURED COVER ARTIST SARA SWOBODA

BODY UNTIL LIGHT
k.m. lighthouse

IT'S JUST YOU & ME, MISS MOON
emily moon

LOVERS AND OTHER STILL CREATURES
eitan codish

2019
FEATURED COVER ARTIST HELLSEA

OTHERWISE, MAGIC
lauren paredes

THE NIGHT SKY IS A PLACE WHERE THINGS GET LOST
andrew chenevert

TIME COUNTS BACKWARD FROM INFINITY
k.m. lighthouse

WE ARE NOT READY FOR WHAT WE ARE
ash good

2018
FEATURED COVER ARTIST HOLGER LIPPMANN

SOUNDS IN MY MÖBIUS MIND
ash good

YOU ARE AN AMBIGUOUS PRONOUN
k.m. lighthouse